Weapons

By Deborah Murrell

WORLD ALMANAC® LIBRARY

Please visit our web site at www.garethstevens.com
For a free color catalog describing Gareth Stevens Publishing's
list of high-quality books call 1-800-542-2595 (USA)
or 1-800-387-3178 (Canada).
Gareth Stevens Publishing's fax: 1-877-542-2596

Library of Congress Cataloging-in-Publication Data

Murrell, Deborah Jane, 1963-
     Weapons / Deborah Murrell.
        p. cm. — (Medieval warfare)
     Includes bibliographical references and index.
     ISBN 13: 978-0-8368-9211-6 (lib. bdg.)
     ISBN-10: 0-8368-9211-9 (lib. bdg.)
     ISBN-13: 978-0-8368-9338-0 (softcover)
     ISBN-10: 0-8368-9338-7 (softcover)
     1. Military weapons—Juvenile literature. 2. Military art and science—
     History—Medieval, 500-1500—Juvenile literature. I. Title.
U810.M87   2008
623.4—dc22   2008016838

This North American edition first published in 2009 by
World Almanac® Library
An Imprint of Gareth Stevens Publishing
1 Reader's Digest Road
Pleasantville, NY 10570-7000 USA

Copyright © 2009 by Amber Books, Ltd.
Produced by Amber Books Ltd., Bradley's Close
74–77 White Lion Street
London N1 9PF, U.K.

Amber Project Editor: James Bennett
Amber Designer: Joe Conneally

Gareth Stevens Senior Managing Editor: Lisa M. Herrington
Gareth Stevens Editor: Joann Jovinelly
Gareth Stevens Creative Director: Lisa Donovan
Gareth Stevens Designer: Paul Bodley

All illustrations © Amber Books, Ltd. except:
AKG Images: 4, 9; Art-Tech/Mars: 11; Board of the Trustees of the Armouries: 12, 14–15;
Bridgeman Art Library: 10 (Bibliotheque L'Arsenal, Paris/Archives Charmet);
Cody Images: 20; Corbis: 6br (Dallas and John Heaton/Free Agents Limited)
24 (Philippa Lewis/Edifice); DK Images: 16; Dreamstime.com: 5; Mars: 3;
Photos.com 6bl, 19; Topfoto: 15br, 18, 21tl and tr.

Printed in the United States of America

2 3 4 5 6 7 8 9 10 09

Contents

CHAPTER 1

Spears, Swords, and Other Weapons

The Middle Ages, or medieval period, began after the end of the Roman Empire in A.D. 476. Many kingdoms in Europe fought for land and power. The men used a variety of weapons. Many of the weapons were the same as those used in ancient times.

Medieval soldiers had to be clever fighters. Survival in war depended on well you could handle your weapons.

Medieval knights also carried spears. They were used for stabbing and were not thrown.

This peasant fought with a sickle, a type of short-handed curved knife that was used for farming.

▶ A BLOODY ATTACK
In this illustration from a medieval **manuscript**, armored soldiers attack a group of peasants.

But the type of weapons a person had depended on his wealth. Poor men often fought only with farm tools and axes. **Noble** knights had many choices of weapons. Many knights could also afford protective equipment, including helmets and **armor**.

Slashing and Stabbing

Medieval soldiers slashed and stabbed using hand-held knives, spears, and swords. Sometimes they used longer weapons, such as **pikes** with sharp points.

Other hand-held weapons, such as **maces**

and **flails**, could knock a man off a horse. A flail could also slam a foot soldier to the ground. A mace was a club with a wooden handle and a metal spiked ball at its end. A flail was similar, but the metal ball was

▼ SPIKED FLAIL
A flail could cause terrible damage. If it was swung with enough force, a flail could crack metal armor and stun an enemy. Flails were hard to control. Sometimes they hurt soldiers as well as enemies.

The flail's handle had a metal disk at the top to protect the user's hand.

Spiked flails did more damage than rounded flails.

A strong chain meant the flail could be swung with great force.

attached to the handle with a chain. Some armies also used spears as throwing weapons.

Sharp Steel

Swords were the main weapon of rich nobles during the early Middle Ages. They were usually made of steel. Steel swords were very costly to make. Nobles fought on horseback. They used their swords for slashing and stabbing enemies. Along with a sharp edge, all swords needed a cross guard. This kept the enemy's sword from

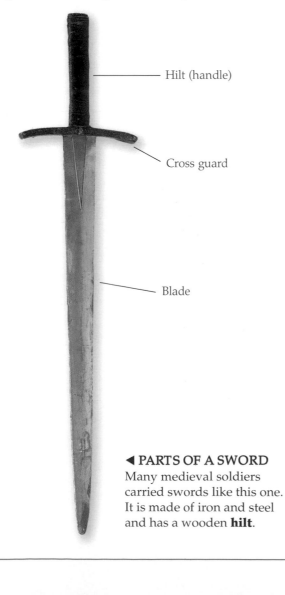

Hilt (handle)

Cross guard

Blade

◄ PARTS OF A SWORD
Many medieval soldiers carried swords like this one. It is made of iron and steel and has a wooden **hilt**.

▲ CROSS GUARD
This close-up of a knight's armor and sword shows the sword's decorated cross guard. It protected the knight's hand from enemy sword blades.

sliding down the blade onto the hand. It also increased the force with which the sword could be swung.

Types of Swords

Nobles from different kingdoms used different shapes and styles of swords. Armies sometimes copied an enemy's weapons, including their swords. As a result, armies often fought with similar weapons. Clever tactics, luck, or greater manpower, and not better weapons, often decided who won a battle.

Sword-fighting Techniques

Knights on horseback could swing their swords downward at enemy troops, causing serious injuries. Knights often repeatedly charged their attackers. That scared the foot soldiers so they would run.

During battles, knights used large swords that they gripped with both hands. These are called **longswords** or "hand-and-a-half" swords. They helped a knight use the force of his entire body in one swing. Not surprisingly, such a blow was deadly. A swing from a longsword could quickly cut off an enemy's head.

▶ MEDIEVAL SWORDS

1 This sword was used by the Vikings, fierce warriors from Scandinavia, in the 800s. It is similar to the swords used by Roman soldiers around 700 years earlier.

2 This one-handed sword is called a **falchion**. It was first used in the 1000s. The falchion was sharpened on one side only, like a modern kitchen knife. It was heavy, like an ax, but much more useful.

3 From the 1300s swords became longer, and so did their hilts. They could be held in two hands. This type of sword became known as a longsword.

4 First used in the 1500s, the **rapier** was a sharply pointed sword with a decorated cross guard. It was used for attacks with one hand, rather than slicing.

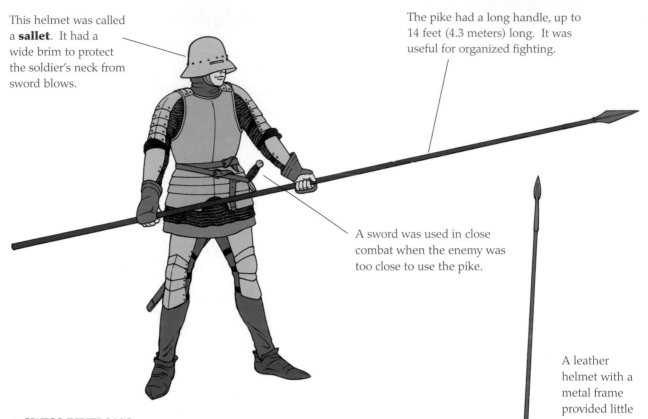

This helmet was called a **sallet**. It had a wide brim to protect the soldier's neck from sword blows.

The pike had a long handle, up to 14 feet (4.3 meters) long. It was useful for organized fighting.

A sword was used in close combat when the enemy was too close to use the pike.

A leather helmet with a metal frame provided little protection.

A cloak kept pikemen warm in cold temperatures.

A small shield was used only for close combat.

▲ SWISS PIKEMAN

This Swiss soldier from the 1500s would have fought on the front line of a battle. The Swiss decided to use pikes after defeating Italian pikemen in 1422. Even though the Swiss won, they were impressed with the weapon and started making their own.

Foot soldiers also used their swords against horses. A soldier might duck under a horse and slash its belly, instantly killing the animal.

Pikes and Spears

Foot soldiers also fought mounted knights with pikes. Pikes are like long spears. Foot soldiers held them against charging knights. They also stuck pikes in the ground with their points directed forward. That often scared the horses and they turned away. The sight of the pointed pikes kept them from

► SCOTTISH PIKEMAN

In the 1300s Scottish pikemen had very little armor. They became known for their bravery because they fought with only a helmet and a shield.

charging. Horses that did not turn away were killed by the sharp pikes.

Pole-axed!

A pole-arm was another weapon used in the Middle Ages. It was a type of ax and spike combined with a hook or spike opposite the ax blade. Pole-arms were often used by foot soldiers to tackle men on horseback. The pole-arm's ax, or spike, could move through armor with powerful force. The Pole-arm's hook could quickly pull a knight off his horse.

Spears in Battle

Long spears were also often used like pikes. At the battle of Taginae (Tag-IN-eye) in 552, an army of Goths, a German tribe, was fighting under their king, Totila. Compared to those of his enemy, the Byzantine (BIZ-zan-teen) leader Narses, Totila's foot soldiers were weak. Totila used his horsemen to repeatedly charge the Byzantine soldiers. The wall of long spears the Byzantine troops had stuck in the ground defeated the Goth horsemen, however, and they fled.

Long spears were always used during the Middle Ages. For instance, the Almogavars, professional soldiers from Spain, used **javelins**, or spears, as their main weapon. A historian in the 1200s described a battle between the Almogavars and the French: *"The Almogavars hurled their javelins [and]... at the first charge more than a hundred knights and horses of the French fell dead on the ground."*

CHAPTER 2

Bows and Arrows

Bows and arrows were used by soldiers as long-distance weapons on the medieval battlefield. Archers loaded their bows, shot their arrows, and reloaded.

The Hand Bow

In the Middle Ages, archers used two main types of bow. The basic type was the **hand bow**. It was made from a single length of curved wood with the two ends strung together. To shoot, the archer or bowman held the bow and pulled the string by hand. Medieval hand bows were very similar to those used today, but were often stronger. It took a great deal of strength to draw, or pull, the string on a medieval hand bow.

▼ ARCHERS ATTACK JERUSALEM
This medieval illustration shows hand bows and crossbows being used by Christians fighting Muslims for control of Jerusalem. The Muslim defenders are also using swords to fight off the Christians (in green) who are climbing ladders to enter the city.

But it could be loaded quickly. The best hand bow could send an arrow up to 300 feet (91 m).

Hand bows came in various lengths. The **longbow**, another hand bow, was about five or six feet (1.5 to 1.8 m) long. It could shoot arrows farther and more exactly than a regular hand bow. The farther the target, the less exact the shot. Because of that, medieval archers did not aim at individual men during battles. They would instead target a certain area and shoot as many arrows at it as quickly as possible. Arrows rained down on the enemy, randomly hitting men and horses.

▼ ARCHER AT AGINCOURT
At the battle of Agincourt (A-jin-CORE), France, in 1415, English archers were an important part of King Henry V's army. The soldier on the left is an English **man-at-arms**. His strong armor, mace, and sword helped him defend the lightly armored archer.

Bows were strung with hemp or flax—two types of natural fiber made from plants.

A longbow was usually as tall as the man who used it. It took great strength and training to correctly draw and shoot a longbow.

A stake stuck in the ground struck the belly of any charging horse.

Arrows were stuck in the ground or kept in a pouch attached to a belt.

Crossbows and Longbows

Another bow used in the Middle Ages was the **crossbow**. It was shorter than a hand bow and easier to carry. Most crossbows had some device to help the archer draw the string back because doing so required such force. A soldier needed great strength—sometimes up to 500 pounds (227 kilograms)—to prepare the crossbow for shooting. A catch in the crossbow's **stock** held the bow in its fully-drawn position. Then the soldier could press the crossbow's trigger, letting go a short arrow, called a bolt, with force.

The part of the crossbow that bends is called the **lath**.

The bowstring was made of strips of cloth.

Pins held a lever in place to allow the crossbow to be drawn.

Stock

Catch and trigger

Wood, **sinew**, and horn were used to make the lath strong and flexible.

Sometimes crossbows were drawn by men who were standing behind those doing the actual shooting. Loaded weapons were sent forward. Empty bows were passed back for reloading. Crossbows were easier to aim than longbows, and could shoot farther — up to 400 feet (122 m).

Even though it was not as powerful as a crossbow, a longbow had some advantages. In 1436 at the battle of Crécy (CRAY-sea), France, the English and French armies fought each other. It began to rain, so the English longbowmen took the strings off their bows to keep them dry. The French

▲ WOODEN CROSSBOW
This German crossbow from 1500 was a deadly weapon for a trained archer.

CHANGES IN CROSSBOW DESIGN

During the Middle Ages, people developed better ways of drawing a crossbow.

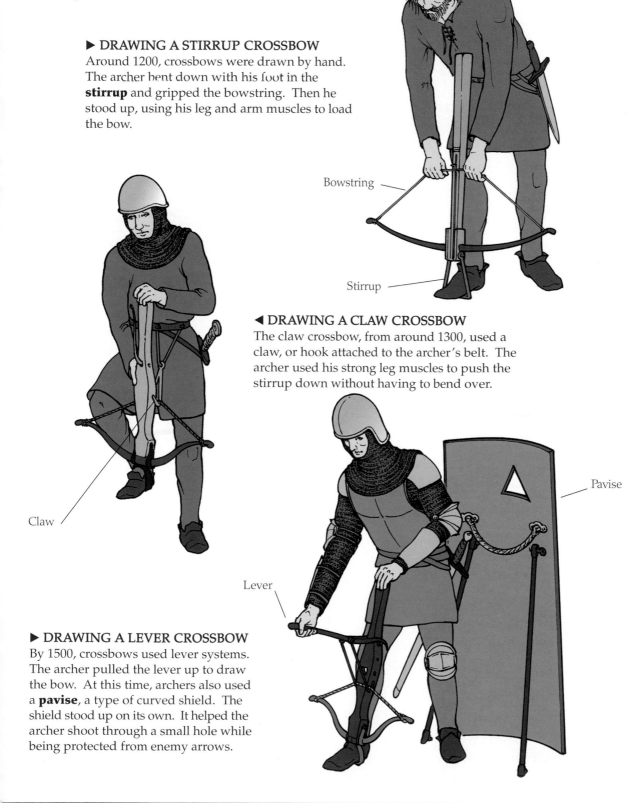

▶ DRAWING A STIRRUP CROSSBOW

Around 1200, crossbows were drawn by hand. The archer bent down with his foot in the **stirrup** and gripped the bowstring. Then he stood up, using his leg and arm muscles to load the bow.

Bowstring

Stirrup

◀ DRAWING A CLAW CROSSBOW

The claw crossbow, from around 1300, used a claw, or hook attached to the archer's belt. The archer used his strong leg muscles to push the stirrup down without having to bend over.

Claw

Pavise

Lever

▶ DRAWING A LEVER CROSSBOW

By 1500, crossbows used lever systems. The archer pulled the lever up to draw the bow. At this time, archers also used a **pavise**, a type of curved shield. The shield stood up on its own. It helped the archer shoot through a small hole while being protected from enemy arrows.

Bolts had feathers at the end known as fletching to help them fly straight. The feathers on this bolt have rotted away.

The shaft was hand cut from a strong, straight piece of wood.

▲ CROSSBOW BOLT
Crossbow bolts were similar to arrows, but shorter and with thicker shafts. This one is shown actual size.

had crossbows, which were harder to take apart. Their strings became wet from the rain, which made them useless. As a result, the English won the battle against a more powerful French force. Crécy was an important battle in the Hundred Years' War between the two kingdoms.

In Their Own Words

*"First the archers began with all their might to shoot **volleys** of arrows against the French. Most were without armor, dressed in their **doublets**, their **hose** loose around their knees, axes, and swords hanging from their belts. Many were barefooted and without helmets."*

—Enguerrand de Monstrelet, Chronicler of the Battle of Agincourt, 1415

Longbow Skills

English armies also became famous for their longbowmen. Skilled English longbowmen were expected to shoot between 10 and 20 arrows per minute. A longbowman might be given 60 or 70 arrows, which would keep him shooting from three to six minutes. Young boys would then bring more arrows to the archers so they could keep shooting.

Shooting the longbow required great strength and skill. Learning how to use a longbow took time. In 1252, King Edward I of England knew that he needed to have good longbowmen ready for future wars. The king ordered that all men in England between the ages of 15 and 60 own at least one longbow. The king outlawed all sports except archery on Sunday. He wanted to make sure that his men practiced shooting.

A sharp bolt head often ripped through armor and caused a deadly wound.

Arrowheads

Arrowheads were normally made out of iron. They came in different shapes. A type of arrowhead known as a bodkin point was very thin and sharp. Bodkin points were the only arrowheads that could kill a knight wearing chain mail, a type of armor made from thousands of connected metal rings. A sharp bodkin point forced open the rings on the chain mail and killed the wearer instantly.

Most arrowheads were attached to the shaft only with wax. When a victim tried to pull the arrow out, the head would come loose from its shaft and stay in his body. Arrows lodged in the body often became infected and caused disease. The safest way to remove an arrowhead was to push it through the body and out the other side. This was very painful.

▶ KING HAROLD KILLED BY AN ARROW
This detail from the Bayeux Tapestry shows the English king Harold being shot in the eye. In 1066, Harold was killed by Norman forces led by William the Conqueror during the capture of England.

CHAPTER 3

Shields and Armor

In the early Middle Ages, few soldiers had armor. Instead they carried large shields, which were sometimes as tall as a man. As armor became more common, and more useful, shields became smaller.

Types of Shields

Shields were usually made of wood and leather. They were easy to carry. Many shields also had a **boss**, or a raised round metal area, in their center. The boss helped enemy blows slide away from the center of the shield. The boss also held a handle on the shield's reverse side, so it could be held in the hand. Because the boss was the toughest part of the shield, it was also a good weapon for hitting an enemy.

Small shields called **bucklers** were also designed for hitting and for self-defense. Bucklers were small enough to be hung from a belt. These shields were useful for hand-to-hand combat. Soldiers used

▶ **WOODEN SHIELD**
This type of shield was used by Viking warriors in the early Middle Ages. It was lightweight and easy to carry.

An iron band around the edge of the shield helped make it stronger.

Colored paint helped locate soldiers on the battlefield.

The shield's boss was made of iron. It could be used to stun an enemy.

Scratches on this shield show that it was used in battle.

bucklers to punch enemies in the face, leaving them stunned. Soldiers often followed the punch with a quick thrust from a sword.

Long shields with rounded tops and narrow bottoms were called **kite shields**. They were useful both on horseback and on foot. When on horseback, kite shields protected the rider's body and leg on one side. These are the shields that Normans used at the battle of Hastings in 1066. The kite shields protected the Normans as they successfully conquered England.

Shield Techniques

Larger shields offered greater protection. They had leather straps on their backs. The straps helped fighters use their lower arms to control the shields. Large shields were too bulky to use on horseback. Instead, foot soldiers used long shields in other ways, often in pairs. For example, one soldier held a shield to protect his partner while he loaded a crossbow. Foot soldiers also connected their shields. Each man's shield overlapped that of the man next to him to form a "shield wall." Sometimes the men

▼ SHIELD FORMATION
Byzantine soldiers defended themselves using a formation called a **foulkon**. Their connecting shields protected them while they fought soldiers on horseback.

Shields protected the face and head from blows from above.

Byzantine soldiers had chain mail to protect the backs of their necks, but they had no other armor.

Spears were held at an angle or dug in the ground. They would have stuck in the belly of a charging horse.

behind the front line of soldiers held their shields over their heads. That protected them against arrows and spears. Some knights used a special shield called a **bouche**. That shield had a cutout shape in the top corner. This was a resting place for the **lance**, which helped make it easier for soldiers to aim.

▼ KNIGHT IN ARMOR

A knight in chain mail is shown in this medieval painting as a Christian saint. Paintings like this were made to inspire medieval knights to fight in the **Crusades**. The Crusades were a series of wars between Christians and Muslims that lasted about 250 years.

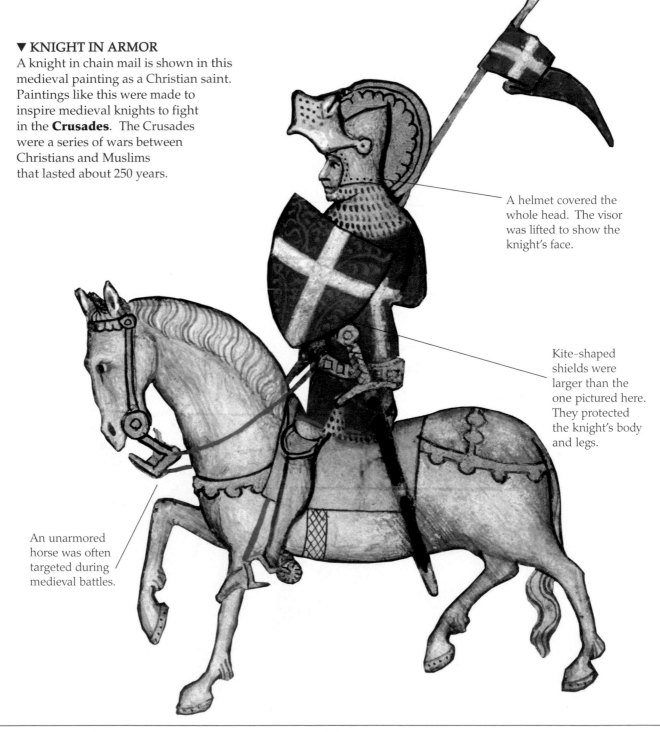

A helmet covered the whole head. The visor was lifted to show the knight's face.

Kite-shaped shields were larger than the one pictured here. They protected the knight's body and legs.

An unarmored horse was often targeted during medieval battles.

Chain Mail Armor

Early medieval armor was made of chain mail. It was made from many tiny metal rings linked together. Chain mail was flexible. Soldiers could move in chain mail easily, but it was too heavy to wear for long periods.

Nobles wore chain mail shirts, called **hauberks**. Nobles also had leather protectors called **greaves** on their shins. Chain mail protected the person wearing it from sword attacks. Chain mail was not useful against direct blows or stabs. For extra protection, people wore a padded vest under the chain mail. That also helped keep their skin away from the scratchy metal.

A chain mail hood was called a **coif**. A noble might also wear a helmet over the

In Their Own Words

"The Byzantines, pushing with their shields and thrusting with their spears, defended themselves most [actively]… and they purposely made a [loud noise] with their shields, terrifying the enemy's horses."

—Procopius, *The Gothic Wars*, 552

coif. Poor people did not have chain mail. Instead of helmets, they wore only leather caps that offered little protection.

▼ CLOSE UP OF CHAIN MAIL
In this piece of chain mail, each metal ring is linked to four others. The design makes it strong and difficult to cut through. A direct blow from a sword, however, would still cause bruising or broken bones.

Plate Armor

From about 1200, metal plates were sometimes attached to chain mail. The armor plates gave extra protection to knees and elbows. A knight may have also worn or **surcoat** (a **tunic** worn over the mail).

In the 1300s, a full coat of plate armor was developed. This was a tunic lined with metal. By the 1400s, nobles fought covered head to toe in full plate armor. It weighed about 50–60 pounds (23 to 27 kg). The armor was heavy, but its weight was spread evenly over the body. Plate armor was more comfortable than chain mail.

Helmets

Not many examples of helmets have been found from the early Middle Ages. They are often only a rounded cap formed from metal strips. Some helmets also had extra strips of metal to protect the nose and cheeks.

Later helmets took many different forms. In Western Europe in the 1100s, fighters wore round helmets made from a single piece of metal. Sometimes the helmets also had a face mask.

DID YOU KNOW?

A mail hauberk was made up of thousands of tiny rings. It took a craftsman weeks to join each ring by hand.

The helmet's visor had only a small slit to see.

Interlocking armor plates let the shoulders and elbows move freely.

A chain mail hauberk was worn under the armor.

Pointed shoes were removed for battle.

▶ SUIT OF ARMOR
This is a full suit of plate armor from about 1480. Only a very rich noble like a king would have been able to afford this luxury item.

Sallets were light, curved helmets with sloped sides. They often had a long point at the back to protect the neck. This German sallet from the 1400s was painted with symbols.

▲ BASINET
This helmet is known as a basinet. It covered the entire head. It had a hinged visor with a small slot to breathe and see. This helmet is decorated with gold. It has a pattern like human hair where the knight's actual hair would have been.

After 1200, helmets changed. A knight on horseback wore a tall, flat-topped helmet called a **great helm**. That helmet was worn when charging an enemy. Later helms often had cone-shaped or rounded tops so that blows from an enemy would slide off the head more easily. The rounded helmets are sometimes called sugarloaf helms.

Another helmet, the **basinet**, began as a smaller helmet worn under the great helm. The great helm was often removed for hand-to-hand combat because it was heavy. It also made breathing difficult. Later, basinets were worn on their own because they fit better and were more comfortable. The German sallet was a helmet with sloped sides that protected the wearer from arrows coming from above.

Horse Armor

Horses also wore armor, usually on the head, chest, and sides. The extra weight meant heavier, stronger horses were needed. Mounted warfare was getting more and more costly. Only the richest knights could afford plate armor and armored horses. They fought in the front lines. Knights with less armor fought farther back.

CHAPTER 4

Fighting Machines

Medieval armies tried to capture castles by laying **siege** to them. That means soldiers surrounded the castle. They attacked castle walls, or tried to force its defenders to give up. If the castle walls could be broken, then the attacking army could get inside the castle. Many machines were invented for attacking castles. The purpose of most machines was to throw stones to break down castle walls. At other times, the attackers might throw objects over castle walls. Often these were grim things, such as the heads of defenders cut off in battles, dead animals, or human waste. Items like this would often spread disease among the people inside the castle. Castle defenders usually gave up if people began dying of disease or hunger.

Giant Crossbow

The **ballista**, or giant crossbow, had been in use since ancient times. It was still common in the Middle Ages. The crossbow shot metal bolts at castles and at their defenders.

▼ BALLISTA
The ballista worked like a large crossbow and shot large metal bolts. It was often used for shooting at castles under siege.

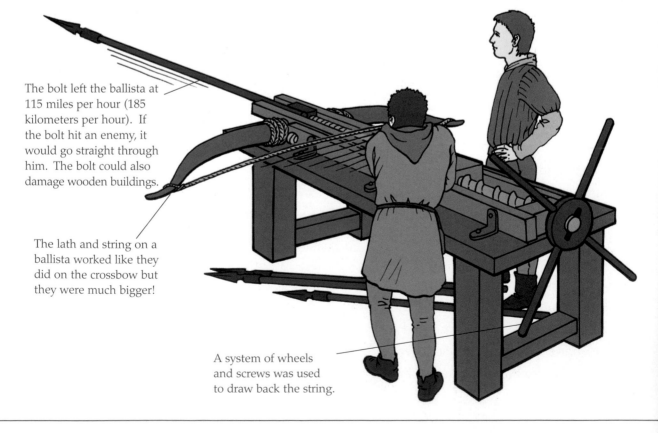

The bolt left the ballista at 115 miles per hour (185 kilometers per hour). If the bolt hit an enemy, it would go straight through him. The bolt could also damage wooden buildings.

The lath and string on a ballista worked like they did on the crossbow but they were much bigger!

A system of wheels and screws was used to draw back the string.

The ballista was drawn by one or more men turning a wheel. Then they would pull a trigger, just like a crossbow.

Slinging Machine

Trebuchets (Tray-BOO-shays) were giant slinging machines. They used ropes and weights to throw heavy stones and other objects. A large trebuchet could send a stone up to 1,200 feet (366 m). In 1218, in a siege at Toulouse in France, women operated the trebuchets. The machines caused great damage to the castle there.

Medieval trebuchets and other machines were huge. In 1304, when preparing to attack Stirling Castle in Scotland, the

▼ LARGE CATAPULT
This machine is called a trebuchet. It worked like a fishing rod does when it is cast. Trebuchets were used to send heavy stones and other objects flying with great speed into castle walls.

The arm of the trebuchet would flick up when the counterweight dropped. That sent the heavy stone hundreds of feet, crashing into castle walls.

A heavy weight pulled sharply down on the arm when it was released.

The lever was used to pull the giant arm down to take a shot.

Stones or rocks were gathered in a strong bag, tied to the rope.

Greek Fire

One of the most powerful weapons trebuchets could throw was Greek fire. That was an oily liquid that exploded into flames on impact. Greek fire burned on any surface, including water. It was almost impossible to put out. The ingredients in Greek fire were kept a secret. Even today we do not know what they were.

English King Edward I built a giant trebuchet called "Warwolf." Although its size is unknown, it took five master carpenters and 49 other workers at least three months to complete. When the Scots saw it, they tried to give up, but Edward knocked down a huge chunk of the castle wall anyway.

▶ BATTLE DAMAGE
Simple machines and Greek fire were used in the siege of Château Gaillard, France, in 1203–1204. Huge stones could tear chunks out of even the strongest castle walls, leaving scars like these.

Stone Throwers

Mangonels were machines that got their power from stretching a rope. They were more flexible than trebuchets because they threw objects out of a "bowl" at the end of a throwing arm. Anything could be put in this bowl, but large stones were most common. Mangonels could throw stones up to 600 feet (183 m) into a castle's walls.

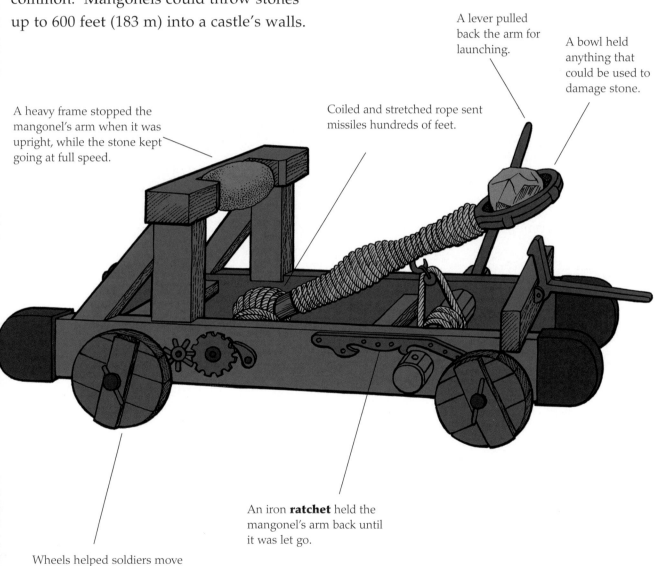

A lever pulled back the arm for launching.

A bowl held anything that could be used to damage stone.

A heavy frame stopped the mangonel's arm when it was upright, while the stone kept going at full speed.

Coiled and stretched rope sent missiles hundreds of feet.

An iron **ratchet** held the mangonel's arm back until it was let go.

Wheels helped soldiers move the mangonel into position.

▲ A MANGONEL
A mangonel was a useful weapon in a siege. Anything placed in its bowl could be thrown hundreds of feet at the enemy. Weapons included stones, burning oil, barrels of Greek fire, and even dead bodies.

CHAPTER 5

Gunpowder

Gunpowder was used in China as early as the 1100s to make fireworks. Gunpowder did not reach Europe until the mid-1200s, but it was soon used in warfare. Armies began using simple cannon as early as 1320. By the 1400s, all sorts of cannon and guns had been invented. Armies moved large cannon to the battlefield on carts. Larger cannon were moved up rivers on **barges**. When the cannon were placed in position, soldiers built special platforms to hold them. Military leaders often used cannon at the beginning of fighting, before hand-to-hand combat.

Cannon

During the late Middle Ages, gunpowder was used by armies to attack forts and castles. Cannon were more effective in breaking down castle walls than earlier machines. Sometimes a single shot from a powerful cannon was enough to make the

defenders of a castle give up. At first, castle owners made castle walls thicker and added more defenses. But new cannon were quickly invented that could smash the thickest stone walls. Soon castles were no longer safe during wartime. Within a short time, fewer and fewer castles were built.

DID YOU KNOW?

Gunpowder is a mixture of charcoal, **sulfur**, and a chemical called saltpeter. In the Middle Ages, saltpeter for gunpowder was made by collecting urine and letting it sit in barrels for a year!

▼ AN ARQUEBUS
An arquebus (AR-ke-buss) was a very early handgun. It was used in the 1400s. An arquebus could blast through plate armor at close range. It was a very loud gun. It also made huge amounts of smoke that frightened and confused horses.

Age of the Handgun

By the second half of the 1400s, handguns became more important than cannon in battle. Early handguns were large, clumsy weapons. Soldiers often fired them from behind special shields to protect gunners from enemy fire. It was easier and quicker to fire a gun than to shoot an arrow from a longbow. With this in mind, military leaders soon replaced archers with gunners.

As the use of cannon and handguns became more common, the era of medieval warfare ended. The Middle Ages, a time of skilled mounted knights and stone castles, drew to a close. When the strongly defended Byzantine capital, Constantinople, fell in 1453 to cannon fire, it was a sign that warfare had changed forever.

In Their Own Words

"The Burgundians shot from behind their [defensive walls] with large, heavy cannon. I saw a few horsemen who were shot in two—their upper body was blown away and their legs remained in the saddle."

—Peter Etterlin on the Battle of Murten (present-day Switzerland), 1476

▼ A SIEGE CANNON

Large cannon like this one were common by the late Middle Ages. Many cannon had protective doors. The door was lowered to protect soldiers from enemy archers while they were loading the cannon. When the soldiers were ready to fire, they raised the door.

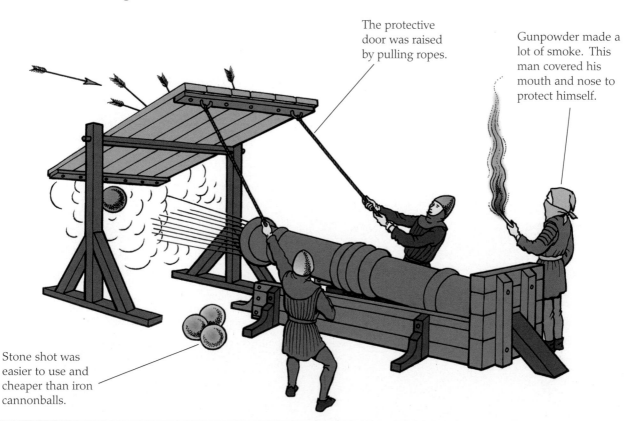

The protective door was raised by pulling ropes.

Gunpowder made a lot of smoke. This man covered his mouth and nose to protect himself.

Stone shot was easier to use and cheaper than iron cannonballs.

1 Sultan Mehmet II sets up camp near Constantinople in April 1453. His army prevents people and supplies from entering or leaving the city.

2 Mehmet's giant cannon, known as the Great Turkish Bombard, pounds the city walls for six weeks. The holes are repaired, but the walls are weakened by the constant **barrage**.

4 Early on May 29, the Turks break through a gate in the outer wall. Their troops pour into the city, killing its defenders. The last Byzantine emperor, Constantine IX, is killed. Constantinople falls to the Turks.

▼ GREAT TURKISH BOMBARD

The sultan's cannon was **cast** in **bronze**. It was made in two pieces: a barrel, and a threaded **breech** section where the gunpowder and shot were loaded. The cannon was 26 feet (8 m) long. It fired granite stones, which each weighed a ton, more than a mile (1.6 kilometers). Each gun was moved into position by 60 oxen and 700 men.

Barrel   A threaded center section screwed the two parts together.   Breech

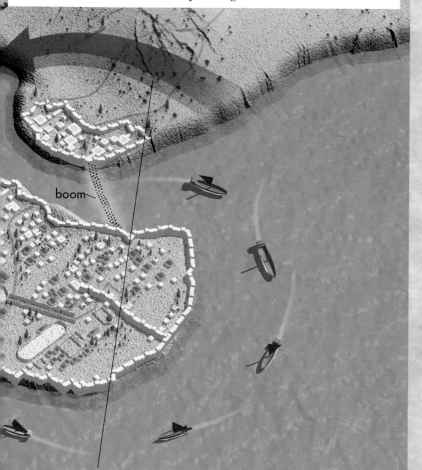

boom

3 The narrow sea passage to the north of the city is defended by a boom, or floating barrier. To get around the boom, the sultan moves his ships over land on giant wooden rollers. Smoke from the cannon hides the defenders' view of the ships. Constantinople is now cut off from the sea on all sides.

The Siege of Constantinople

1453

The cannon was an important medieval invention. In fact, cannon fire was the main instrument behind the greatest siege of the Middle Ages—the capture of the great walled city of Constantinople (Istanbul).

Constantinople was the capital of the Christian Byzantine Empire, which by 1453 was in crisis. The city was almost surrounded by the armies of the Ottoman Turkish leader, Sultan Mehmet (MEM-et) II. Mehmet wanted to make the city the new capital of his Muslim empire.

The End of an Empire

The siege of Constantinople was the first time that heavy cannon had been used to attack a walled city. Sultan Mehmet used huge cannon to break down the city's thick walls. The walls were built more than 1,000 years earlier. People thought they were unbreakable. But cannon fire proved to be stronger than stone. It was the beginning of a new age. The use of gunpowder would decide the outcome of all future battles.

Glossary

armor—clothing worn to protect soldiers in battle

ballista—a weapon like a giant crossbow used to throw lances or spears

barges—large boats with a flat bottoms used to carry freight or heavy weapons

barrage—a heavy attack against an enemy using weapons such as cannon

basinet—a close-fitting metal helmet, with a visor

Bayeux Tapestry—a medieval embroidered cloth that celebrates the successful invasion of England by William of Normandy in 1066

boss—a metal stud in the center of a shield

bouche—a shield with a notch cut into the top corner where a lance could be rested and aimed

breech—an opening at the back of a gun barrel or cannon where the ammunition is loaded

bronze—a metal made from copper and tin

bucklers—small, round shields

cast—to pour molten metal into a mold

coif—a hood made out of chain mail

crossbow—a small bow with an instrument for drawing strings and releasing arrows

Crusades—a series of wars between European Christians and Muslims in the Holy Lands, a region today known as the Middle East

doublets—tight-fitting padded jackets

falchion—a broad, slightly curved sword sharpened on one side only

flails—weapons made of wooden shafts with short heavy sticks attached to them

foulkon—a defensive fighting technique used against soldiers on horseback in which shields are joined and spears are dug into the ground

great helm—a metal helmet that covered the head

greaves—leather or metal armor pieces worn below the knees to protect the calves and shins

hand bow—a hand-drawn bow for shooting arrows

hauberks—knee-length shirts of chain mail

hilt—the handle of a sword

hose—close-fitting leggings worn by men

javelins—light spears thrown by hand

kite shields—large shields that were wider at the top than at the bottom

lance—a long wooden weapon with a pointed metal tip carried by soldiers on horseback

lath—the part of a crossbow which bends when it is drawn, usually made of wood

longbow—a large hand bow

longswords—large swords designed to be used with both hands

maces—clubs with wooden shafts and heavy metal or stone heads that were used as weapons

man-at-arms—a well-trained and well-armed soldier who was paid to fight

mangonels—machines for throwing stones and other objects using tension in ropes or other materials

manuscript—a document written by hand

noble—a member of the wealthy ruling class

pavise—a large shield with a stand to hold it up and a small hole for an archer to shoot through

pikes—long spears used by foot soldiers

rapier—a light, sharp sword used for thrusting

ratchet—a mechanical device used to prevent a shaft from turning, or to make it turn in one direction only

sallet—a light metal helmet with a flared brim

siege—the surrounding of a town, city, fortress, or castle by an enemy army in order to capture it

sinew—animal tendons

stirrup—metal, leather, or wooden loop designed for a soldier to put his foot in while drawing a crossbow

stock—the straight part of a crossbow in which the lath and release instrument are attached

sulfur—a yellow, non-metallic chemical element used as an ingredient of gunpowder

surcoat—an outer coat worn by a knight over armor

trebuchets—large machines used for slinging stones and other missiles

tunic—a loose, thigh-length piece of clothing similar to a dress, often without sleeves

volleys—groups of arrows released at the same time

For More Information

Books

The Bayeux Tapestry. David Mackenzie Wilson (Thames & Hudson, 2004)

Knights & Castles. Insiders (series). Philip Dixon (Simon & Schuster Children's Publishing, 2007)

Knights, Castles, and Warfare in the Middle Ages. World Almanac Library of the Middle Ages (series). Fiona MacDonald (World Almanac Library, 2005)

Medieval Weapons and Warfare: Armies and Combat in Medieval Times. The Library of the Middle Ages (series). Paul Hilliam (Rosen)

Medieval Warfare. Medieval World (series). Tara Steele (Crabtree Publishing, 2003)

The Norman Conquest of England. Pivotal Moments in History (series). Janice Hamilton (Twenty-First Century Books, 2007)

Web Sites

Castle & Siege Terminology
http://home.olemiss.edu/~tjray/medieval/castle.htm
Search a glossary of terms that describes the features of medieval castles. Find out about turrets, parapets, weapons, and much more.

Castles of Britain: Castle Learning Center
http://www.castles-of-britain.com/castle6.htm
Tour this fascinating site. It contains articles, photographs, artwork, and diagrams explaining medieval life, including information about castles and weaponry.

The Medieval World: Medieval Battles
http://medieval.etrusia.co.uk/battles
Learn more about medieval England, its castles, knights, warfare, and the Crusades.

The Middle Ages
http://www.learner.org/interactives/middleages
Charge through this site and learn about the feudal system, religion, castles, clothing, and the arts.

Index